D1510286

Productions in Print
An In An Hour Book
www.inanhourbooks.com
An imprint of Smith and Kraus Publishers, Inc.
Published by Smith and Kraus, Inc.
177 Lyme Road, Hanover, NH 03755
www.SmithandKraus.com

Copyright © 2010 by Sarah Treem.
All rights reserved.

First Fig, Second Fig © 1922, 1950 by Edna St. Vincent Millay;
I, being born a woman and distressed © 1923, 1951
by Edna St. Vincent Millay and Norma Millay Ellis.
Reprinted by permission of Holly Peppe, Literary Executor,
The Millay Society.

CAUTION: Professionals and amateurs are hereby warned that *THE HOW AND THE WHY* is subject to a royalty. It is fully protected under the copyright laws of the United States of America and of all countries covered by the International Copyright Union (including the Dominion of Canada and the rest of the British Commonwealth), the Berne Convention, the Pan-American Copyright Convention and the Universal Copyright Convention, as well as all countries with which the United States has reciprocal copyright relations. All rights, including professional, amateur stage rights, motion picture, recitation, lecturing, public reading, radio broadcasting, television, video or sound recording, all other forms of mechanical or electronic reproduction, such as CD-ROM, CD-I, information storage and retrieval systems and photocopying, and the rights of translation into foreign languages, are strictly reserved. Particular emphasis is laid upon the matter of readings, permission for which must be secured from the Author's agent in writing.

All inquiries concerning rights, including amateur rights, should be addressed to:

SUBIAS
C/O MARK SUBIAS
ONE UNION SQUARE WEST, NO. 913
NEW YORK, NY 10003
212.445.1091 (phone)
212.898.0375 (facsimile)

Manufactured in the United States of America.

THE HOW
and
THE WHY

By **Sarah Treem**

Emily Mann
Artistic Director

Timothy J. Shields
Managing Director

• About McCarter Theatre Center •

Tony Award-winning McCarter Theatre Center, located in Princeton, New Jersey, is recognized as one of the foremost performing arts centers in this country to serve as both a professional producing theater and a major presenter of the performing arts. McCarter achieves this distinction by commissioning, developing, and producing ambitious new works that infuse the national and international repertoire with fresh vitality, while also creating provocative and original productions of classic plays and modern masterpieces. Beginning with the world premiere of Thornton Wilder's *Our Town* in 1938, McCarter Theatre has consistently launched significant productions whose impact is felt long after the closing performance. Ultimately, McCarter strives to create work that engages in the questions of our time, producing stories that resonate across cultural divides and fostering dialogue between world events and the work on our stages.

For more information, visit **www.mccarter.org**.

• About the Playwright •

SARAH TREEM (*Playwright*) is the only writer to have written and produced all three seasons of the acclaimed HBO series, *In Treatment*, for which she won a WGA award and was nominated for a Humanitas award. She is also a writer/producer for the Mark Wahlberg/Stephen Levinson produced HBO series *How to Make it in America* and is currently adapting Samantha Peale's novel *The American Painter Emma Dial* for HBO with Philip Seymour Hoffman and Emily Ziff. Sarah participated in the 11th annual Tel Aviv-Los Angeles Film and TV Master Class in Israel in July 2009 and in a conference titled "How They Did It: Turning an Israeli series into HBO's *In Treatment*" for New York Women in Film & Television in March 2010. Her full-length plays include *Empty Sky; Against the Wall; Mirror, Mirror; A Feminine Ending;* and *Human Voices. A Feminine Ending* received its world premiere at Playwrights Horizons in fall 2007, was subsequently produced at South Coast Repertory and Portland Center Stage in 2008, and is published by Samuel French, which has also published *Mirror, Mirror. Human Voices* was part of Manhattan Theater Club's Spring Boards New Play Series and New York Stage & Film's Powerhouse Reading Season in 2007. Sarah has been in residence at The Sundance Institute, The Ojai Playwriting Conference, The Screenwriters Colony, and will soon be in residence at the Yaddo Artists' Colony. She has been commissioned by South Coast Repertory and Playwrights Horizons, and she is a current fellow at the Lark Playwrights' Workshop. Sarah has taught playwriting at Yale University, where she earned her B.A. and M.F.A.

• Artistic Director's Note •

There are some scripts one simply can't put down—they grab you, and you must go along for the ride. I will never forget the first time I read Sarah Treem's *The How and the Why*. I knew—almost immediately—that I had a smart and profound, thought-provoking and funny, sublime and brilliant new play in my hands. And I knew that McCarter's audience absolutely had to see it.

The How and the Why is a play about sex and gender, power and age, nature and nurture, loss and love. It is a play that compels us to examine some of the unexplored questions of what it is to be a woman—biologically, socially, politically, and emotionally. It is also a great relationship play—a play about two women of different generations, desperately trying to find a common ground. Sarah's dialogue is sharp and her characters complex; but most of all, her ideas are challenging—both intellectually and emotionally.

I first met Sarah several years ago when she was a student, working for her MFA at the Yale School of Drama. We shared a car ride and a discussion and found a shared set of artistic ideals and values. Since then, Sarah's career has grown tremendously—she's had her plays produced around the country, and she now serves as a writer and supervising producer for HBO's acclaimed series, *In Treatment*. Hers is an important voice that will continue to be heard in the American theater; and I'm thrilled that McCarter's audience will be the first to see this wonderful, engaging, and absolutely unforgettable play.

EMILY MANN

• Playwright's Note •

I began *The How and the Why* in reaction to a couple of different things. I had a very smart boyfriend at the time, who read a book called *Woman* by Natalie Angier and he passed it on to me and said, "I think you'd like this." The entire book is fascinating (it's a comprehensive study of female physiology), but there were two theories that stuck with me after I finished it. One was about menopause. The other was about menstruation. That book was the intellectual impetus for this play. Emotionally (and I believe that all good plays flow from both places), I had just opened my first play in New York. I was 27. The play got slammed by the paper of record. From the time I was very young, I had only ever wanted to be a playwright, so that was devastating for me.

But, since I'm a dramatic writer, I paid close attention, as the experience was unfolding, to my response and the responses of those near to me. I remember being surprised that some of my harshest critics were women. I thought I had been writing in service of womanhood. In significant distress, I finally sat down with a very powerful woman—a theatrical producer—and I asked her how one sustains a life in theater. (By that point, I had begun working in television, which I really enjoyed, but my heart was committed to the stage.) So I asked this woman for her advice. And she told me, in a tough love sort of way, to stop writing plays about women.

Now, as former mentors of mine can attest, when someone tells me to do something, I usually do the opposite. (I don't recommend that strategy, by the way.)

So I began thinking about what it meant for my generation to be the daughters of the great feminists. What it meant, for me, to be the daughter of my own mother. What it meant to be a woman. An intellect. A girlfriend. And a conversation started to develop in my head. Between a mother and daughter. Both whip-smart. Both ambitious. Who are equally desperate for and terrified by each other.

I have to say, I am very grateful to have written this play. Not because I think it's a perfect play, but because it seems to open the door to some very exciting conversations. Nobody tells you, when you're young (or, at least, nobody told me), that there is no right or wrong way to go about life. For the most part. For the most part, there are no right or wrong choices. As the character Zelda says in the play, "You're a scientist, he's a scientist. You have the kids. He has the kids. It really is a tree of possibilities, isn't it?" There are a million different ways to be human, and while that was initially somewhat upsetting information, once I got comfortable with the idea, it became electrifying. Over the course of working on this play, with Emily, Mercedes and Bess, and others, in earlier forms of development, I have had the opportunity to glimpse myriad roads through these woods. And, my god, that's made me feel less alone.

SARAH TREEM

THE HOW
and
THE WHY

McCarter Theatre produced Sarah Treem's *The How and the Why* in January 2011. It was directed by Emily Mann with set design by Daniel Ostling, costume design by Jennifer Moeller, lighting design by Stephen Strawbridge, and sound design by Robert Kaplowitz. The producing director was Mara Isaacs, the director of production was David York, the casting director was Laura Stanczyk, CSA, the dramaturg was Carrie Hughes, and the production stage manager was Alison Cote. The cast was:

Zelda Kahn......................Mercedes Ruehl
Rachel Hardeman......................Bess Rous

The playwright would like to thank: Mercedes Ruehl and Bess Rous; Robin Swicord, Nick Kazan and Zoe Kazan; Deb Levine; Rodrigo Garcia; Stockard Channing; Alison Pill; Kathleen Chalfant; Tracee Chimo; Kelly McGillis; Celia Keenan-Bolger; Blair Brown for the inspiration; David Weiner and David Huang, for being the ones I trust; My friend, Mark Subias; Tim Sanford; Chris Sumption; Playwrights Horizons for the commission; Hedgebrook and the Ojai Playwrights Conference for the development; Carrie Hughes, Dan Rubenstein, everyone at McCarter, and of course, my hero, Emily Mann; My grandmother, Bena, for her wit; My father, Will, for his mind; My brother, Jon, for his heart; And Alec, for the book and the faith.

Please note: This script was published prior to the opening performance at McCarter Theatre, and may not reflect final revisions.

For my mother,
who is sometimes my mirror
and sometimes my map.

Time

Present. Late autumn.

Place

A Senior Professor's office in Cambridge, MA.
Later, a dive bar in Boston.

Characters

Rachel Hardeman, 28, evolutionary biologist. Graduate
student at NYU. Emotional. Excitable. Brilliant.

Zelda Kahn, 56, evolutionary biologist. Senior professor at
Harvard. Reserved. Cynical. Brilliant.

Note: These women think and speak quickly. And talk about
science as easily as they would talk about the weather.

The How and the Why was originally produced by
McCarter Theatre Center, Princeton NJ.
Emily Mann, Artistic Director; Timothy J. Shields, Managing Director;
Mara Isaacs, Producing Director

The How and the Why was commissioned by Playwrights Horizons with
funds provided by Kate and Samuel Weingarten.

Scene One

Zelda is behind an elegant mahogany desk, pouring over an unbound manuscript and checking it against a few heavy tomes open before her.

The office is dark, auspicious and very masculine.

Rachel enters hesitantly through the open door.

She watches Zelda for a long time. Zelda remains oblivious.

Finally Rachel inches forward, with surprising silence. She stands in front of the desk like an errant pupil.

Zelda looks up and freezes.

ZELDA

Oh, my God.

RACHEL

Hi, I'm Rachel.

ZELDA

I'm Zelda. It's a pleasure to meet you.

Rachel offers her hand. Zelda accepts it. Holds it a moment too long.

ZELDA

Oh, I'm sorry.

RACHEL

That's okay.

ZELDA

Won't you sit?

RACHEL

Thank you.

Rachel sits. Silence.

ZELDA

When did you arrive?

RACHEL

Just now.

ZELDA

Did you take the bus? Or the train?

RACHEL

My boyfriend drove me.

ZELDA

Oh, is he outside?

RACHEL

No, he went into town. He's going to pick me up in a bit.

ZELDA

I see. So how long have I got you for?

RACHEL

We're staying in town. I can come back.

ZELDA

Oh. Wonderful.

Silence.

RACHEL

So thanks for seeing me. I hope I didn't freak you out or anything.

ZELDA

Freak me out?

RACHEL

By just calling, out of the blue.

ZELDA

You didn't freak me out. I've been waiting for that call for quite some time now.

RACHEL

I wasn't ready until recently.

ZELDA

Please, don't explain, that will only make things worse.

RACHEL

Make things worse?

ZELDA

For me, I mean, not for you.

> *Beat.*

RACHEL
confused

I'm sorry, have I offended you?

ZELDA

What?

RACHEL

Do you want me to leave?

ZELDA

What? Are you insane? Please sit.

> *Rachel doesn't move.*

ZELDA

Or, if you prefer, I'll stand.

> *Zelda stands up. Rachel doesn't know what to make of this. Maybe she laughs. Maybe she just sits in a chair across from Zelda.*

> *Zelda sits too.*

ZELDA

There. Isn't this nice? So. How should we begin?

RACHEL

Begin?

ZELDA

How would you like to proceed?

RACHEL

I... I don't know.

ZELDA

I would assume you've given it some thought.

RACHEL

Of course, I've —

ZELDA

Do you have questions you'd like to ask me?

RACHEL

I have a million, but —

ZELDA

The way I see it, your areas of curiosity must be divisible into the historical, the biological, and the psychological.

RACHEL

Would it... would it be okay if we just sat here for a second?

ZELDA

Of course.

They sit in silence. Staring at each other.

RACHEL

I like your office.

ZELDA

Thank you.

RACHEL

It feels very… masculine.

ZELDA

You mean it feels significant.

RACHEL

No, I don't.

ZELDA

Yes, I believe you do.

More silence.

ZELDA

So, did you take the train or the bus?

RACHEL

No, my boyfriend / drove me.

ZELDA
overlapping

Your boyfriend drove you. That's right. I must have had a small stroke.

That was a joke, though at my age I really shouldn't kid.

Oh dear, you look frightened. Forget I said anything.

You are very beautiful.

RACHEL

I know.

ZELDA

Oh.

RACHEL

I'm sorry.

ZELDA

No, that's — it's good that you know.

RACHEL
I'm sorry, I'm terrible at compliments.

ZELDA
I understand, so am I.

RACHEL
Plus, I'm so fucking nervous.

ZELDA
quietly

So am I.

Would you like a drink?

RACHEL
It's ten AM.

ZELDA
Yes, I suppose that is a little early.

RACHEL
What have you got?

ZELDA
Champagne. Seems appropriate.

RACHEL
Okay.

> *Zelda opens a cabinet to reveal a little refrigerator and full bar. She pulls out a champagne bottle.*

ZELDA
My colleagues gave this to me the day I won a big honor in my field called the Dobzhansky Prize. I've been saving it for just the right occasion.

> *Zelda pops the cork and pulls out two flutes. She fills both a little too high and hands one to Rachel.*

L'Chaim.

RACHEL

What are we toasting to?

ZELDA

To life.

> *They clink glasses and drink. Rachel looks around the office.*

ZELDA

I'm sorry it's such a mess. We're hosting a big conference here this weekend for NOORB — the National Organization of Research Biologists — it's like the Olympics of Biology — and we've been frantic, trying to prepare for it.

> *Rachel just nods.*

ZELDA

You said you're a scientist too? On the phone?

RACHEL

Yes, I am. I'm a grad student at NYU.

ZELDA

Fantastic. Chemistry? Physics?

RACHEL

Biology, actually.

ZELDA

Biology. You're kidding. What are the odds? Molecular, I assume? That's the hot specialty these days. Inner space, as it were. Of which, I am blissfully ignorant —

RACHEL

Evolutionary.

                          ZELDA

Evolutionary biology?

                          RACHEL

Yes.

                          ZELDA

As in, my field?

                          RACHEL

I know, right? What are the odds?

> *Beat. Zelda stares at Rachel.*

                          RACHEL

So I, of course, know all about the NOORB conference this
weekend.

                          ZELDA

You're a graduate student in evolutionary biology at NYU.

                          RACHEL

I am.

                          ZELDA

That is extraordinary.

> *Uncomfortable silence. Rachel looks around the room.*

                          RACHEL

Who said that?

                          ZELDA

Sorry?

                          RACHEL

That quote on your wall.

                          ZELDA

Ah.

Zelda goes to her wall and pulls off a little wooden plaque.

ZELDA
reading
"My candle burns at both ends;
It will not last the night;
But ah, my foes, and oh, my friends —
It gives a lovely light!"

RACHEL
It sounds familiar. Is it Byron?

ZELDA
No.

RACHEL
Tennyson.

ZELDA
Vincent.

RACHEL
Who?

ZELDA
Edna St. Vincent Millay.

RACHEL
A woman wrote that?

ZELDA
You sound surprised.

RACHEL
It just sounds so… ballsy.

ZELDA
She was, by all accounts. Vincent Millay.

                    RACHEL
Who is M?

                    ZELDA
Sorry?

                    RACHEL
"With love and admiration—"

                    ZELDA
Oh yes, M. Um, that would be Michael.

                    RACHEL
Who's Michael?

                    ZELDA
My… boyfriend.

                    RACHEL
You have a boyfriend?

                    ZELDA
It's a little ridiculous, I know, at my age.

                    RACHEL
What does he do?

                    ZELDA
He's an oncologist.

                    RACHEL
He sounds smart.

                    ZELDA
He is.

                    RACHEL
                    a joke
So we both have smart boyfriends. There. That's something
in common.

    Zelda smiles. They both relax. A bit.

ZELDA

Your boyfriend's name is?

RACHEL

Dean.

ZELDA

Is he very handsome?

RACHEL

I think so.

ZELDA

That's good. With a name like Dean it would be a shame if he weren't.

The office phone rings.

RACHEL

Do you want to get that?

ZELDA

No, that's alright I—I'll just let them—in fact—

Zelda picks up the ringing phone and replaces it on the receiver, effectively hanging up on the caller.

RACHEL

What if that was important?

ZELDA

Nobody calls this landline but pesky students. If it were important, they would know to call my—

Zelda's cell phone starts to ring on the desk.

ZELDA

—cell.

Zelda checks the caller ID.

I'm terribly sorry, would you mind if I just —

RACHEL

Of course.

Zelda answers the call.

ZELDA

Hello? Hello, Darling. It's not a great time, I'm with… oh, I see. No, that's alright, just tell me quickly… I see… Yes, of course. Vienna it is, then… I'm looking forward to it, I really am… Yes, I'll call you later to discuss all the logistics… Alright, you too.

Zelda hangs up.

ZELDA

Speak of the devil.

RACHEL

Was that Michael?

ZELDA

Yes.

RACHEL

He's taking you to Vienna?

Beat.

ZELDA

He is indeed.

RACHEL

When?

ZELDA

After NOORB.

RACHEL

That's so nice.

He's a nice man.

For a moment, Zelda is distracted. Lost. Rachel watches her, carefully.

ZELDA

I'm sorry, I—this is *really* an extraordinary day.

What were we just discussing? Before I—was it your research?

RACHEL

My research? No.

ZELDA

Well, perhaps it should be.

RACHEL

You want to hear about my research?

ZELDA

A good place to begin. A rather neutral topic, isn't it?

RACHEL

Not to me.

Zelda stops. Puts her hand on her heart. Looks at Rachel.

RACHEL

Are you alright?

ZELDA

I'm fine... just give me a moment.

I am so glad you said that. I feel the same way.

RACHEL

I applied to the NOORB conference.

ZELDA

You did?

                         RACHEL
I didn't get in.

                         ZELDA
Which one was your abstract?

                         RACHEL
Which one?

                         ZELDA
I read some of the submissions —

                         RACHEL
Why?

                         ZELDA
I'm on the board.

        Beat.

                         RACHEL
I didn't know that.

                         ZELDA
You should have. You should be familiar with whomsoever
is on the board of all the conferences you apply to. That's
just good sense.

        Beat. Rachel is offended.

                         RACHEL
Uh, it was about human menstruation.

                         ZELDA
That was *your* abstract?

                         RACHEL
You read it?

                         ZELDA
Not personally, no, but I certainly heard of it. It was — well, it
was rather famous actually, among the post-docs —

RACHEL

Famous in a bad way?

ZELDA

What? No, no. I don't know. It sounds like it shook people up.

RACHEL

Why wasn't it selected then?

ZELDA

I'm sorry?

RACHEL

If everyone was talking about it, why didn't you give it a slot in the conference?

Beat.

ZELDA
gently

An abstract needs two champions on the selection committee to even be reviewed by the board.

RACHEL

And mine didn't have that?

ZELDA

No, if I remember correctly, it only had one.

Beat.

RACHEL

Who?

ZELDA

Uh. A former student of mine. A woman named Bethany Gillette.

RACHEL

Never heard of her.

Beat.

                          ZELDA

You're upset.

                          RACHEL

I'm not.

                          ZELDA

You are and that's good. It's good that you're upset.

                          RACHEL

I just think your selection process kinda sounds like bullshit.

                          ZELDA

You're quite right.

    Tense silence.

                          ZELDA

Yes, well, perhaps it was naïve of me to think that science could be our neutral topic. But wait! We weren't talking about research at all. We were talking about men. Let's return to that. They're much less incendiary.

    Rachel smiles. They both relax. A bit.

                          ZELDA

Tell me about yours.

                          RACHEL

Dean?

                          ZELDA

How long have you been seeing each other?

                          RACHEL

Three years.

                          ZELDA

And what does Dean do?

RACHEL

He's a scientist.

ZELDA

Oh dear.

RACHEL

He's not like the rest of them.

ZELDA

Uh-huh.

RACHEL

No, really. You'd never know he was a scientist.

ZELDA

I'd know.

RACHEL

We're in the same program. At NYU.

ZELDA

So he's your age?

RACHEL

A year younger, actually.

ZELDA

Good. That's very good.

Again, Zelda seems lost. For a moment. In another world. Pause.

ZELDA

Are you planning to marry him?

RACHEL

No.

ZELDA

Why not?

RACHEL

Neither of us believe in the institution.

ZELDA

What's to believe?

RACHEL

Dean's parents divorced before he was born. Then they both married again and divorced again, so he doesn't think he has the gene for it.

ZELDA

And your parents?

RACHEL

They're dead.

ZELDA

You're kidding.

RACHEL

I wouldn't kid about something like that.

ZELDA

No, forgive me. I'm sorry, I just—I didn't know.

RACHEL

How would you?

ZELDA

When did they die?

RACHEL

Five years ago. I was in college.

ZELDA

Was there an accident or—?

RACHEL

No. They were just old. He died of lung cancer. And then, she followed him, like a year later.

She just kind of… lost her will to live.

ZELDA

I'm so sorry, Rachel.

Rachel shrugs.

RACHEL

You never married, did you?

ZELDA

Ah, no, never.

RACHEL

Yeah, what's the point? It's so much more romantic to wake up every morning and know you're both there by *choice*. Not because you're bound together by law.

Zelda studies Rachel carefully.

ZELDA

So he's your guy? This Dean?

RACHEL

Absolutely. He's my guy.

ZELDA

You should marry him then. Make it official.

RACHEL

I just told you—I don't see the point of the institution.

ZELDA

I'll tell you the point. Tax cuts. And health benefits. Which may not seem significant to you now, but trust me, later on, especially once children enter into the picture—

RACHEL

Excuse me?

ZELDA

If you're certain—if you're absolutely certain that Dean is the only man you will ever want to be with—and sleep with—for the rest of your life, then do yourself a favor and get hitched. It will save you a fortune.

Beat. Rachel stares at Zelda.

ZELDA

It's just my opinion.

RACHEL

Which I didn't ask you for.

ZELDA
surprised

I'm afraid I offended you.

RACHEL

You didn't.

ZELDA

You look angry.

RACHEL

You don't know me. Maybe this is my happy face.

Why would I want *your* opinion? I don't even know why I'm telling you this. It really isn't any of your business.

ZELDA

Rachel—

RACHEL

Please, don't—don't call me that.

ZELDA

It's your name.

RACHEL

Yes, but it suddenly sounds… bizarre coming from you.

ZELDA

Bizarre, how?

RACHEL

Creepy, alright? It sounds creepy.

ZELDA

What should I call you?

RACHEL

Just don't… don't call me. This was a mistake. I have to go.

ZELDA

Where are you going?

RACHEL

I have to go call my lab. When I left New York this morning, I put one of my undergrads in charge of changing the saline solutions and I think he was high, so—

ZELDA

My dear girl—

RACHEL

I am *not* your girl.

ZELDA

Ms. Hardeman. How's that?

Pause.

RACHEL

That's fine.

ZELDA

Suitably formal?

                          RACHEL
Yes.

                          ZELDA
Please sit down.

                          RACHEL
No.

                          ZELDA
Jesus. This is quite difficult.

                          RACHEL
Did you expect it to be easy?

                          ZELDA
Well, I think I'm trying a bit harder than you are.

                          RACHEL
Which is appropriate, isn't it?

    Beat.

                          ZELDA
I didn't mean to offend you. I am simply amazed by the
options you seem to have before you. Marry him, don't
marry him. You're a scientist. He's a scientist. You have the
kids. He has the kids. It really is a tree of possibilities, isn't
it?

    Rachel is still standing. She looks towards the door.

                          ZELDA
I thought maybe you'd like to see some pictures.

                          RACHEL
Pictures?

ZELDA

You know, of other people, family members? Me, when I was younger?

RACHEL

No, thank you. This has been strange enough. I don't need to spend the rest of the morning gazing upon Zelda Mildred Kahn, age ten.

Rachel holds out her hand. Zelda rises slowly, takes it.

ZELDA
carefully

I hate my middle name.

RACHEL

Yeah, it's pretty bad.

ZELDA

I try never to reveal it. You must have done some sleuthing.

Rachel gathers her bag, puts on her coat —

RACHEL

Not really. It's in your bio.

ZELDA

Which bio did you read?

RACHEL

The one on the conference website.

ZELDA

Posted under "Board Members?"

Rachel freezes.

RACHEL

Shit.

ZELDA
I thought you didn't know that I was on the conference board.

RACHEL
Yes. I just remembered that too.

Silence.

RACHEL
I lied.

ZELDA
I gathered.

RACHEL
I do that sometimes.

ZELDA
Good to know.

RACHEL
Should I leave?

ZELDA
Would you like to?

RACHEL
I feel like I should.

ZELDA
I'd rather you stayed.

Beat. Rachel sits down again.

ZELDA
delighted
You're really something of a terror, aren't you?

                         RACHEL
Charles says I'm difficult.

                          ZELDA
Who's Charles?

                         RACHEL
Sorry. Charles Byrne. My advisor at NYU. Do you know
him?

                          ZELDA
I've heard of him. How is he?

                         RACHEL
Oh, he's fantastic.

                          ZELDA
He sounds a bit patronizing.

                         RACHEL
Not at all.

                          ZELDA
He called you difficult.

                         RACHEL
You called me a terror.

                          ZELDA
But the word "terror" suggests a certain ferocity, someone to
be contended with.

   Rachel shrugs.

                          ZELDA
I myself acquired a reputation for being difficult in my
youth. Though, back then I think the clinical term was
"bitch."

RACHEL
If you were a man, you would have been celebrated for it.

ZELDA
But I'm not a man. Neither are you.

I know it seems romantic in your youth to behave badly —

RACHEL
Who said I behave badly?

ZELDA
Charles said "difficult" —

RACHEL
Because I refuse to sleep with him. That's what he means. Difficult to fuck.

Beat.

ZELDA
Well. You certainly seem to have it all figured out.

Uncomfortable silence.

ZELDA
Is there anything you want to ask me, Rachel? Anything at all?

Rachel thinks.

RACHEL
What's it like to win the Dobzhansky prize?

Zelda is taken aback.

ZELDA
Uh, it's a thrill, of course.

RACHEL
You got it for the Grandmother Hypothesis.

ZELDA

I did, yes.

RACHEL

How old were you?

ZELDA

Young. Your age.

RACHEL

You were 28?

ZELDA

29.

RACHEL

Fuck.

ZELDA

Excuse me?

RACHEL

I'm so behind.

ZELDA

It's not a race.

Beat. Rachel stares at the award.

ZELDA
kindly
Why don't you tell me about your research?

RACHEL
You don't want to hear about my research.

ZELDA
Why not?

RACHEL

Because it kinda contradicts your research.

ZELDA

amused

Do you think I'm scared?

RACHEL

Maybe.

ZELDA

My dear. I have thirty years of ground-breaking data behind me, dozens of publications, grants and a handful of global awards that are very difficult to come by. You have, by all accounts, an interesting idea. Believe me, I want to hear it.

RACHEL

It's a very powerful idea.

ZELDA

Aren't they all.

RACHEL

It's going to change everything.

ZELDA

And by "change everything" you mean it's going to add another minor wrinkle into the incredibly cavernous foreheads of the couple dozen research biologists that actually bother to read scientific journals and can summon enough energy to care about a hypothesis that isn't their own.

RACHEL

No, I mean it's going to change everything. The way that women think about their bodies. The way that men think about women's bodies. The way that people have sex.

ZELDA

It's going to change the way people have sex.

RACHEL

Yes.

ZELDA

Well. Don't make me beg.

Rachel looks at Zelda, suspiciously.

ZELDA

I'm past the age where I have any interest in intellectual supremacy. These days, I'm simply looking for the truth. You might have it.

Silence.

RACHEL

You know Ernst Mayr, the evolutionary biologist?

ZELDA
smiling

I do.

RACHEL

Well, he said that in biology, every issue is understandable from two perspectives—the how and the why. The mechanism and the function. The immediate explanation and the eternal one. In the case of female menstruation, we know the how. We know an egg drops down from one of the ovaries, hangs out in the uterus, waiting for a sperm, and if none comes, the uterine lining sheds, and it, along with the egg, gets flushed through the vagina in a monthly bloodbath. We know how it happens. But we don't know why.

Beat. Rachel looks at Zelda. Zelda doesn't say anything.

And we've never cared. Because for hundreds of years professional scientists have been exclusively male and they don't menstruate so they don't care. But every aspect of our physiology has evolved for a reason. And the reason that we menstruate has never been obvious to me. It doesn't make sense. It's so calorically expensive to shed an endometrial layer every freaking month. And for our prehistoric predecessors, who spent their whole lives malnourished, every calorie counted.

Do you want to respond?

ZELDA
confused
You haven't said anything yet.

RACHEL
Menstruation also limits the window of opportunity for conception, which is the holy grail of evolution. So the benefit of menstruation has to somehow outweigh this tremendous cost.

Again, Rachel stops. Again, nothing from Zelda.

RACHEL
Do you disagree?

ZELDA
With what?

RACHEL
With my theory.

ZELDA
You haven't yet stated a theory.

RACHEL
Menstruation is a defense.

Against what?

RACHEL

The toxicity of sperm.

Silence.

ZELDA
impressed

My God, that's ballsy.

RACHEL

Think about it. Sperm are riddled with foreign matter, just by virtue of being the products of another person's body, not to mention all the microbes — bacteria, viruses, and parasites that men are carrying around on the tips of their rods and women have buried in their bush. You put a sperm under a microscope, do you know how much other shit you find hanging on? The little pimp has a pathogenic entourage. And they all get a free ride up into the poor defenseless uterus. It's like some pristine, glacial lake, away from everything and then in come the sperm and bam! Oil spill. So what do we do? We clean ourselves out. Every month, we flush. Get rid of the old, infected endometrial tissue. Grow something new.

Say something.

ZELDA

That's quite a theory.

RACHEL

Why is there a flow of blood? You can slough dead tissue without bleeding. Our skin cells flake all the time. But to change the uterus, we have to bleed. Why?

ZELDA

To loosen the dead cells of the uterine layer.

RACHEL

If it was purely mechanical, our bodies could use water. But what does blood carry?

ZELDA

Immune cells.

RACHEL

Exactly. T cells, B cells. Macrophages that act like internal Windex and clean the shop. But why get rid of all that tissue? Why not just reabsorb it like we do with the lining of our stomachs? Because it's not good to reabsorb *infected* tissue. And now, here's the kicker. Why, when compared to other female mammals, is the human menstrual flow so much heavier?

ZELDA

Because we're bigger.

RACHEL

We're not bigger than gorillas.

ZELDA

Because we have more pathogens in our uteruses.

RACHEL

And why would we have more pathogens?

ZELDA

Because we have more sex.

RACHEL

Exactly. Right. We fuck all the time—not just in heat. Not just to reproduce. We build up more pathogens. We bleed for a long period of time.

ZELDA

So, by this theory, sexually active women have heavier periods?

RACHEL

Probably, but the differential would be too negligible to quantify. The real test, I believe, lies in comparing the menstrual output of one species of primate to another and then evaluating the results in comparison to the sexual proclivity of the respective species.

ZELDA

What'd you find?

RACHEL

The data's inconclusive. Menstruation in nonhuman animals hasn't ever been studied systematically.

ZELDA

Have you conducted any of your own experiments?

RACHEL

No. I don't have access to monkeys.

ZELDA

The girl who read your abstract, Bethany? She's a former student of mine. She's down at the Yerkes Primate Center at Emory studying the childbearing practices of chimps. And bonobos, I think. The two of you must meet.

RACHEL

That would be great.

ZELDA

Do you know if the concentration of pathogens is most intense in a woman's uterus right before menstruation?

RACHEL
I assume it is.

ZELDA
But do you have the data?

RACHEL
They've proven menses is preceded and accompanied by a massive infiltration of pathogen-fighting immune cells into the endometrium in studies by Jones from 1930, Nugent from 1935, Gardley from 1950, Kaufold from 1980 —

ZELDA
That's not what I asked.

RACHEL
Do I have the data that proves that pathogen concentration is higher right before menstruation? Of course not. That's an incredibly invasive experiment that's never been done. It would involve sticking a probe into the uteri of hundreds of sexually active women, multiple times a month. Who's going to authorize that?

ZELDA
Also, you must have considered the fact that most prehistoric women spent their entire adult lives continually pregnant —

Rachel is looking at Zelda, strangely.

ZELDA
What's wrong?

RACHEL
It sounds like you've thought all of this through before.

ZELDA
I have, of course.

RACHEL

And yet, you've never published anything about it.

ZELDA

About why women menstruate? I've never had anything worth publishing. In all my years of considering the physiology of the female reproductive system, I've never stumbled upon such a remarkable hypothesis.

Pause.

RACHEL

Then you think I'm on to something.

ZELDA

Frankly, I think it's a bit revolutionary.

RACHEL

I thought it was a good idea. I mean—I was hoping—it came to me in a dream. I *knew* it was a good idea.

Rachel starts to cry.

ZELDA

Is something wrong?

RACHEL

No.

Rachel puts her head down on the table. Zelda reaches out a hand. It hovers above Rachel's hair for a moment, then Zelda pulls it back.

RACHEL

I just get a little emotional sometimes when I talk about my hypothesis. Charles says if I ever win the Dobzhansky Prize, he's going to give me a Xanax before the ceremony so I don't embarrass myself.

Rachel wipes her eyes.

RACHEL

Do you have a tissue?

Zelda takes out a box of tissues and passes it to Rachel.
Rachel blows her nose.

ZELDA

I feel like this is going badly.

RACHEL

Let's be honest. Maybe there was no way it could have gone well.

ZELDA

I really like your hypothesis.

RACHEL

Thank you.

ZELDA

This little theory might very well make you famous, Rachel.

RACHEL

Not if it never gets published.

Pause.

ZELDA

There's an open slot, actually.

RACHEL

What?

ZELDA

At NOORB. I just heard this morning. One of our presenters dropped out, so there's a spot available in the morning of the second day.

RACHEL

What are you saying?

ZELDA

I'm asking, if you'd like to—

RACHEL

You can't do that.

ZELDA

Do what?

RACHEL

You can't just offer me a presentation.

ZELDA

Why not?

RACHEL

Doesn't the whole board have to approve me?

ZELDA

Well technically, yes, but I don't think that will be a problem. I'll vouch for you.

RACHEL
confused

As your daughter?

ZELDA

No. As a new member of the scientific community to whom I give my endorsement.

It's a somewhat radical theory and it might be helpful to have the approval of somebody a bit older before you—well, throw yourself to the wolves, really.

I'd want to read the whole abstract. Unless, of course, you feel it isn't ready—

RACHEL
quickly

It's ready. That would be—I would be—I just need to run it by Dean, but I think we would both be thrilled.

ZELDA

Who's Dean?

RACHEL

My boyfriend.

ZELDA

Yes, of course—and you want to check with him because...?
No, nevermind. That's none of my business.

RACHEL

We were going to do it together.

ZELDA

Do what together?

RACHEL

Present my abstract. At NOORB.

Beat.

ZELDA

What?

You do realize it's highly unorthodox for anyone who didn't
author the abstract to present it before a national conference
of this magnitude.

RACHEL

What's the big deal?

ZELDA

The big deal is people will think Dean created your
hypothesis. Which isn't true.

Is it?

RACHEL

We bounce all our ideas off of each other.

ZELDA

Who came up with the theory of menstruation as a defense against the toxicity of sperm?

I thought it came to you in a dream.

RACHEL

Are you saying you won't introduce us both?

ZELDA

If Dean gets up on that podium with you, people are going to think of you two as one scientific mind.

RACHEL

That's okay with me.

ZELDA

It shouldn't be.

RACHEL

I get really anxious when I speak in public.

ZELDA

So take a beta blocker.

RACHEL

I'll present something solo the next year.

ZELDA

What makes you think you'll get in next year?

RACHEL

Then the year after.

ZELDA

Rachel, this theory is a revelation. Many scientists slave away their entire lives and never come close to anything like it.

RACHEL

And I dreamed it up at twenty-eight. So there'll be others.

Jesus.

RACHEL

Why does it matter so much to you? You like the theory, right? You said you liked the theory. Why does it matter who stands behind the podium?

Zelda just stares at Rachel.

RACHEL

I'm not worried about my career. I've already co-authored three articles with Charles for *Science* magazine. I won the Ruth L. Kirschstein award from the NIH. I also won the National Science Foundation's postdoctoral fellowship for next year. I'm going to be fine.

ZELDA

And how's Dean doing? In the program?

RACHEL

He just co-created a groundbreaking new theory on the evolutionary imperative of hominid menses.

ZELDA

And otherwise?

He's in danger of being cut, isn't he?

Rachel looks at Zelda.

RACHEL

Can I smoke in here?

ZELDA
surprised

You smoke?

RACHEL

Yes, sorry. It's a disgusting habit. I hate myself. Can I crack a window?

ZELDA

Be my guest.

> *Rachel gets up, goes to a gothic window and opens it. She takes out a pack of cigarettes, lights one and inhales. Zelda watches the whole event, fascinated.*

ZELDA

You do realize that's a known carcinogen, right?

RACHEL

I've heard.

> *Zelda crosses to the window seat to join Rachel. Rachel offers her a cigarette.*

ZELDA

I quit.

> *Rachel rolls her eyes. Takes another drag. And relaxes. A little bit.*

RACHEL

Dean has one of the best minds at the lab. But nobody knows that because Dean doesn't speak up. He's shy. And he hasn't hit upon that one thing yet that will make his career —

ZELDA

And time is running out.

RACHEL

People expect it to take women longer. If I don't hit anything for another three or five or ten years, it's fine. In fact, if I hit it any earlier, they're liable to get suspicious. Who was helping me? Whose idea is this, really?

ZELDA

That's not as true as you'd like it to be. A good idea is a good idea. You have a good idea. People will see that, regardless of your gender, regardless of your age.

RACHEL

I couldn't have done it without Dean.

Zelda sighs.

RACHEL

He teased it out with me. Came at it from another angle. He made it watertight.

ZELDA

It's not watertight. Nothing is.

RACHEL

Will you introduce us both? Or just me?

Zelda doesn't say anything.

RACHEL

He works so hard. He deserves a little recognition in his field. I know you think I'm committing some sort of heinous crime, but I know what I'm doing. I want a family. I want children. I want a full life. I don't want to end up alone with my research in thirty years.

ZELDA

Like your mother.

Beat.

RACHEL

That's not what I'm saying. I didn't say that. I wasn't talking about you.

I'm sorry.

ZELDA

You seem very much in love.

RACHEL

I am.

ZELDA

I never married.

RACHEL

I know.

ZELDA

Why do you think I never married?

RACHEL

Because you cherished your independence.

ZELDA

Yes. And because nobody ever asked. When I was young, I made it clear that I didn't need anybody in my life. I took lovers, I left lovers. Old, young, men and women—I saw myself as an explorer. A sexual Magellan. I was not particularly good at monogamy, but in those days, nobody was. And I was lucky enough, as a young woman, to make an important discovery, which led to eventual tenure and financial security. So I didn't need to marry anyone to take care of me.

RACHEL

You're preaching to the choir. I'm not getting married.

ZELDA

And your Dean agrees?

RACHEL

Oh, yes. He never wants to get married.

ZELDA

This equation doesn't add up. You don't want to marry him, but you're happy to wed him to your discovery. So you will be united, at least in the professional sense.

RACHEL

You're reading too far into this.

ZELDA

There's nothing wrong with wanting to marry the man you love.

RACHEL

I don't want to marry him!

ZELDA

You don't want to marry him or he doesn't want to marry you?

Silence.

RACHEL
stunned

You don't even know me.

ZELDA

Why doesn't Dean want to get married? Have you ever asked him?

RACHEL

He wants to build up a career first. Get published. Win a fellowship or two. He wants to be able to support me. And I respect that. I'm willing to wait.

ZELDA

Or you can just hand him the discovery right now. Speed the whole thing up.

RACHEL

That's not what I'm doing.

Are you sure?

RACHEL

First of all, it's just a theory. A *theory*. And second of all…

Rachel stabs out her cigarette and stands up.

RACHEL

Fuck you. I should go.

ZELDA

I know this is uncomfortable.

RACHEL

Uncomfortable?

ZELDA

We all lie to ourselves to get through our lives. And then every so often, somebody comes around and hands us a magic mirror. It's a gift, really, though, at the time—

RACHEL

A magic mirror? Look, I've enjoyed meeting you. Forget about presenting me, or Dean, at the conference. If I didn't get in, I didn't get in. I don't need a favor from *you*.

Rachel gathers her things.

ZELDA

Whose name was on the abstract?

RACHEL

What?

ZELDA

I'm just curious, since I never saw the application itself, did it list both your names?

Rachel starts for the door.

ZELDA
quietly, urgently
You've come up with a really good idea. It took rigor, it took study, it took courage and it took genius. And it is *yours*. You created it. You *gave birth to it*. Don't give it away because you're frightened of the implications. It is yours. Keep the damn thing!

Rachel stops at the door.

RACHEL
What about Dean?

ZELDA
Dean's big moment will come later. It sounds like he needs a little longer to grow into himself. Into his own ideas. You're wrong about the gender politics of science. Because he is a man, his window of opportunity will be longer, not shorter.

RACHEL
He is all I have.

ZELDA
That's not entirely true, is it?

RACHEL
Yes. My parents are dead. The only person who gives two shits about what happens to me is Dean.

Pause.

ZELDA
What about your work?

RACHEL
My *work?*

ZELDA

You don't appreciate it—you can't appreciate it now. You're too young. But trust me. It will save you. It will lift you and it will hold you ten feet above whatever tempest descends. It is your life-vest, it is your therapy, it is the fountain of fucking youth. You have been blessed. Believe me. *Believe me.*

He'll understand. If he's as good a man as you say he is, he'll be happy for you. That's the key to surviving together in this field. You celebrate each other through success, support each other through failure, but you do not entangle alliances. And you do not compromise.

RACHEL

Does the Grandmother Hypothesis keep you warm at night?

ZELDA

As a matter of fact, it does.

Rachel is still at the door. She doesn't know what to do.

RACHEL

You can't do that.

ZELDA

Do what?

RACHEL

Come back into my life, after 28 years, and say "I'm your mother. *Believe me.*"

ZELDA

My dear, you found me.

What should I say?

I've never done this either, Rachel. Tell me what you want to hear.

Silence. Rachel crosses back.

RACHEL

I read the Grandmother Hypothesis on the ride up. Your original paper.

ZELDA

My God. Why?

RACHEL

I've only studied it through secondary sources. It's such a polarizing theory. I wanted to know what you actually wrote.

ZELDA

What did you think?

RACHEL
confused

Well... I didn't realize premature reproductive senescence wasn't identified until the fifties.

ZELDA

It's true.

RACHEL

So before then, nobody had noticed that human beings are the only primates to go through menopause?

Zelda shrugs.

ZELDA

I'm sure they noticed.

RACHEL

But they hadn't bothered to study it.

ZELDA

George Williams came up with a theory, around that time, that said, because it takes human children so long to grow up, their mothers had evolved to live longer.

RACHEL
confused
That's not how evolution works.

Zelda smiles.

ZELDA

I know. But back then, if anyone bothered to ask the question, that was the party line.

RACHEL

Until you went to study the Hadza.

Zelda laughs.

ZELDA

No, until the mid-seventies, when the guys finally became interested in estrogen.

RACHEL

Because given, post-menopause, it seemed to prolong a woman's life.

ZELDA

Right. So then, suddenly, everyone was curious — if estrogen is so good for women, why do their bodies stop making it?

RACHEL

Which brought menopause as an evolutionary imperative under scrutiny?

ZELDA
disgusted

Exactly. Because if estrogen is the life-force, then what were post-menopausal women still doing alive? Maybe it was just a lucky break. The consequence of modern medicine. Maybe they're all just lame ducks.

RACHEL

Have you ever read the *Nascence of Senescence*?

ZELDA

Henry Mortimer's paper? Of course. It's seminal.

RACHEL

The Grandmother Hypothesis basically repudiates it.

ZELDA

Well, it's also wrong.

The *Nascence of Senescence* states that prehistoric woman died off when their eggs did. That is simply not true. I had the proof.

RACHEL

This proof… it was the Hadza?

ZELDA

That's right. They're primordial. Nomadic. They speak in clicks. They're as close as we come to a community living under Pleistocene conditions in modernity and yet, they experience menopause. Those women routinely live into their seventies.

RACHEL

So menopause is natural.

ZELDA

I think so.

RACHEL

But "the why" still remains. What's the point?

ZELDA

The point is simply this. Prehistoric women were continually pregnant. But childbearing is exhausting and breastfeeding is so calorically expensive that a woman would have barely been able to eat enough to keep her infant alive. She would have had no time or energy to forage for her older children. For those children to reach maturity, they needed another guardian. A woman without responsibilities towards her own offspring.

RACHEL

A grandmother.

ZELDA

A grandmother, correct. So the lucky women who lived longer in the Pleistocene epoch helped their grandchildren reach maturity. Thus, their gene pool thrived. And adapted towards longer life.

RACHEL

Which eventually allowed us to evolve beyond monkeys?

ZELDA

Precisely. Monkey mothers breastfeed their children for four or five years, but after that, they won't peel them a fucking banana. The simian child grows strong and stays stupid because his brain becomes concentrated on finding food. But the human child, who has a grandmother to peel his bananas, can stay weak and grow smart. His brain can continue to develop. He can think complex thoughts. So in a sense, when women started raising their children's children, they invented childhood, which in consequence, created humanity.

Pause.

RACHEL

That's actually a fucking gorgeous theory.

ZELDA

Thank you.

RACHEL

And you tell it so well.

ZELDA

I've had thirty years to get comfortable talking about it. One day you'll feel the same way about your hypothesis. After you've defended it to thousands of people, it becomes like an old lover. Someone you fell for years ago, when you were young and stupid.

Beat.

RACHEL

You did your post-doc work at Columbia, right?

ZELDA

That's right.

RACHEL

Who was your advisor?

Beat.

ZELDA

Henry Mortimer.

RACHEL

That must have been awkward.

Zelda shrugs.

ZELDA

Max Gluckman called science "any discipline in which the fool of this generation can go beyond the point reached by the genius of last generation."

RACHEL

Aren't you and Mortimer in the same generation?

ZELDA

No! He's almost twenty years older.

I have great respect for Henry Mortimer. In many ways, the relationship you have with your advisor sounds a lot like the relationship we had.

RACHEL

But you didn't stay at Columbia.

ZELDA

No. That's true. I didn't.

Silence. Zelda doesn't offer anything more. Rachel checks her watch.

RACHEL
genuinely

It was… wonderful to meet you. I really have to go now. Dean is waiting for me.

ZELDA

They are going to want to dismiss you too. They will look for any excuse. I have been fighting for thirty years, with everything I have, to get people to listen to the Grandmother Hypothesis. To take seriously the claim, by a woman, that Adam never lost a rib. That we are not biologically, from a purely scientific standpoint, secondary. We are smaller, yes. We are weaker, yes. Our brains contain less mass, true, true, true. And yet, *we live longer.* And that is not an accident. That is evolution.

You have no idea the work it has taken just to be heard, never mind believed. And the sacrifices I've—but… I got here. And now, when I talk, people listen.

RACHEL

Was it worth it?

Beat.

ZELDA

I was too young to raise a child.

RACHEL

How old were you?

Beat.

ZELDA

Twenty-eight.

RACHEL

Okay. I guess we're different that way.

> *Rachel puts out her hand to shake once again. Zelda grasps it, fervently.*

ZELDA

But nobody is asking you to give up a child. All I'm asking you to do is give yourself a chance. You're standing right where I was—

> *Zelda holds up Rachel's hand.*

ZELDA

With a theory in your palm that will liberate women from the shame of menses. And you're about to hand it off to your lover to keep peace in your bed.

> *Rachel yanks her hand back.*

ZELDA

And you're too young to know that it's one of those mistakes you will never recover from.

I want to read you something.

> *Zelda goes to the bookcase, pulls out a book and opens it.*

ZELDA
reading

I, being born a woman and distressed
By all needs and notions of my kind,
Am urged by your propinquity to find
Your person fair, and feel a certain zest
To bear your body's weight upon my breast:
So subtly is the fume of life designed,
To clarify the pulse and cloud the mind,
And leave me once again undone, possessed.
Think not for this, however, the poor treason
Of my stout blood against my staggering brain,
I shall remember you with love, or season
My scorn with pity, — let me make it plain:
I find this frenzy insufficient reason
For conversation when we meet again.

Zelda looks up at Rachel, expectantly.

RACHEL

Edna again?

Zelda nods.

RACHEL

Honestly Zelda, she sounds like a woman who has never
been in love.

Zelda closes the book, sadly.

ZELDA

Where are you going?

RACHEL

Home.

                    ZELDA
Back to New York?

                    RACHEL
I guess.

                    ZELDA
You're not going to stay through NOORB?

                    RACHEL
I wasn't invited.

                    ZELDA
I will get you that slot. If it's you up at that podium or Dean
or both of you. It is a good idea. It deserves to receive the
greatest possible attention.

    Beat. The women just look at each other.

                    RACHEL
Thank you.

                    ZELDA
You have three days to prepare.

                    RACHEL
I know.

                    ZELDA
Would you like to meet again? There are a few other things
I'm unclear about.

                    RACHEL
Like what?

                    ZELDA
Well, for example, blood contains iron, which is one of the
things bacteria needs to proliferate. So wouldn't all that
menstrual blood promote uterine infection, rather than
dissolve it?

RACHEL

It would, unless our bodies had created some way to sequester the iron. Such as immune cells secreting lactoferrin in high density to bind to the iron and make it unusable to bacteria. And it just so happens, in a 1978 study, plasma levels of lactoferrin were found to be twice as high in the endometrium right before menses than during the mid-cycle.

Rachel smiles at Zelda.

ZELDA

I have other questions.

RACHEL

Ask them at the Q & A. It will give me a way to quiet the thunderous applause.

Rachel goes.

Zelda sips her champagne.

Lights down.

A break.

Mercedes Ruehl in *The How and the Why*

All photos by T. Charles Erickson

Mercedes Ruehl and Bess Rous in *The How and the Why*

Mercedes Ruehl and Bess Rous

Bess Rous in *The How and the Why*

Scene Two

A dive bar.

Rachel is waiting there, nervously. She keeps looking at her watch.

She stands up to leave.

Zelda walks in.

She spots Rachel, waves, and comes over to her table.

ZELDA

I'm so sorry I'm late.

RACHEL
cold

It's okay.

ZELDA
nervous

It's not okay. I shouldn't have kept you waiting. I seem to be late to everything lately. I don't know where my mind is. I almost missed my flight back from Vienna because I—oh never mind, it's not important. Do they serve food here? I'm starving.

Rachel just stares at her.

ZELDA

You do eat, don't you dear? I've been meaning to ask you that. Do you eat? Because you look thin. And perhaps that's your natural body type. But it isn't my natural body type and it wasn't your father's, so I've been meaning to ask you, do you eat?

RACHEL

What's my father's body type?

Beat. Zelda looks at Rachel.

ZELDA
Later. Later we will discuss your father. And his body type.
And his sexual proclivities, if you're interested, which you
may not be. But first, we must order food. Though, I gained
seven pounds in three days in Vienna. Between the bread
and the lard and cream sauce and all that pig product. I
don't know how the Austrians stay so thin. Actually I do.
They smoke like chimneys.

Zelda looks around the dingy little space for a waiter.

ZELDA
I used to be thin like that, when I smoked.

RACHEL
How much did you smoke?

ZELDA
About a pack a day.

RACHEL
A pack a day?

ZELDA
Yes, and I regret every second of it. You must quit.

Zelda can't find a waiter anywhere.

RACHEL
How did you quit?

ZELDA
I got pregnant. What are you drinking?

RACHEL
Bourbon.

ZELDA

Wow. You really can drink. You didn't get that from me. But perhaps I'll have some wine. They do serve wine here, don't they?

RACHEL

It's probably from a box.

ZELDA

From a box? That's outrageous. Waiter!

Zelda is just signaling into the ether. Rachel rolls her eyes.

RACHEL

You have to go up to the bar and order it.

ZELDA

Charming.

Zelda starts to rise. Rachel shoots the rest of her bourbon down.

RACHEL

I'll get it. White or red?

ZELDA
bewildered

White.

Rachel gathers her empty glass and goes to the bar.

Zelda tries to make herself at home. The place is much dirtier than she's used to.

Rachel returns with two drinks.

She sits.

ZELDA

Thank you.

RACHEL

How was Vienna?

ZELDA

How was Vienna. Well, Vienna, from what I saw of it, was amazing. Like a little city out of time. And the Austrians… they're so… rational. They are observational empiricists, every one. Really, it was just heaven. If you and Dean ever have the opportunity to go, I'll give you the name of the little inn where I stayed. I had a room in the attic.

RACHEL

How's Michael?

Beat.

ZELDA

He's good. Lovely man.

RACHEL

I thought he might propose to you there.

ZELDA

Propose? For heaven's sake.

RACHEL

Why else do people fly off to Vienna for a weekend?

ZELDA

He didn't propose.

RACHEL
not sorry

I'm sorry.

ZELDA

Don't be.

A beat. Zelda raises her glass.

RACHEL

What are we drinking to?

ZELDA

To you, my dear. And your achievement at the conference.

RACHEL

My achievement?

ZELDA

The speech was quite spectacular. Beautifully articulated. Gloriously original. And brave. Really, most of all, terrifically brave. The room around you just crackled. Did you feel that?

Beat.

RACHEL

They hated me.

ZELDA

I don't think that's true.

RACHEL

It's not really a matter of opinion.

ZELDA

Everything is a matter of opinion. You think our senses are to be believed? There's no such thing as heat. There is the experience that we have when we touch something we perceive as hot. But heat itself is not a thing. The same applies to criticism.

RACHEL

Have you been reading the blogs?

ZELDA

The what?

RACHEL

The scientific blogs. On the Internet?

ZELDA

No.

RACHEL

I've read at least a dozen blog posts in response to the NOORB conference.

ZELDA

If all these people are blogging, who is running their labs?

RACHEL

One blog talked about the "horror show" that was Rachel Hardeman's NOORB presentation. Another said if NOORB was so desperate for female presenters this year, they would have been better off asking a high school science teacher to discuss what her students had discovered in their petri dishes. Because that presentation would, presumably, have been grounded in some form of reality. Another said he couldn't pay attention to my talk because the name I had given my primate prototype reminded him of a porn star.

ZELDA

What was her name again?

RACHEL

Bloody Mary.

ZELDA

What kind of porn is he watching?

> Beat.

RACHEL

Does it matter?

ZELDA

That was a joke.

Rachel, welcome to the game. You wanted to play with the big boys — this is how they play.

RACHEL

That's not true. I've been to these conferences before. I've seen the criticism lobbied against other hypotheses. This was worse. They were specifically vicious towards me.

ZELDA

You don't think you're being a little paranoid?

RACHEL

No.

ZELDA

Why would they be specifically vicious towards you?

RACHEL

Because I am a woman.

Beat.

ZELDA

Rachel, don't.

RACHEL

They dismissed me. They never even engaged my argument. They didn't consider it. I walked up there, in my skirt and my heels. I said sperm and pathogen in one sentence. I said menstruation and defense in another and they all stopped listening. I saw them stop.

ZELDA

You *saw* them stop *listening*.

RACHEL

Yes, and then, they went after me *personally*. Not my theories, my right to have them. They had done their homework. At the cocktail hour afterwards, these two board members came up to me and they basically implied that if I had known my father, I might be less suspicious of sperm.

ZELDA
confused

That doesn't make any sense.

RACHEL

I know! And do you know what they'd have to do to find out I was adopted? They'd have to hire a private investigator!

ZELDA

I don't think anyone did that. Everyone's bio gets printed in the conference program.

RACHEL

My bio doesn't say that the people who raised me were not my direct genetic predecessors.

ZELDA

I might have brought it up to the board.

RACHEL

What?

ZELDA

I just mentioned it, in passing, when I was pitching you. As another indication of how significant your trajectory has been.

RACHEL

What?

Everyone was so impressed by your abstract and how young you are, that they wondered if perhaps you came from a family of scientists. So I said no... that I knew you a bit personally... and that you were adopted —

RACHEL
hurt
You said you "knew me a bit personally"?

ZELDA

Yes.

Pause.

ZELDA

Is there a problem with that?

Rachel doesn't answer.

ZELDA

Anyway, if you'll allow me to give you a piece of advice — *do not* turn the reaction to your hypothesis into an issue of sexism, not in your own mind, and certainly not in public. It will do nothing for you. You're worried about being discredited? *That* will discredit you.

RACHEL

I've already been discredited.

ZELDA

Stop it. No, you haven't. You presented a very progressive theory to a national organization at an annual conference and it received mixed responses. It is an honor to have presented at the conference at all, and if you don't do anything stupid, you have the rest of a lengthy career to recover.

RACHEL

To *recover?*

ZELDA

I mean, to review your hypothesis and make improvements.

RACHEL

I thought you loved my hypothesis.

ZELDA

I like it very much. I do.

RACHEL

You just said it needs improvements.

ZELDA
frustrated

You are twenty-eight years old! You don't think you have anything left to learn?

Silence.

ZELDA

Were you able to hear — to really hear any of the questions the audience asked?

RACHEL
incredulous

You think I should have changed Mary's name?

ZELDA

One pointed out that monthly menstruation is a modern phenomenon. Because our ancestors were constantly pregnant or amenorrheic, so they didn't need to expel their uterine lining. Which, when last we met, was something I suggested you really should consider —

RACHEL

I did consider it.

ZELDA

Why hadn't you prepared a defense?

RACHEL

I had.

ZELDA

Well… why didn't you share it when he asked the question?

RACHEL

He didn't ask a question. He just made a statement and then, if you remember correctly, there was a cacophony of applause. Applause! But before I could tell them why it was the most overly simplistic, reductionist response to what I had proposed, some other fifty-year old, balding asshole jumped up with another dogmatic "question," which I again wasn't given the opportunity to respond to. And then, of course, there was Bethany.

ZELDA

Ah yes, Bethany. Well, if we're considering things through your worldview, that was a stroke of very bad luck. If we're considering things through mine, and I sincerely hope we soon will be, it could also have been the opportunity for a really lively debate. Who knew Bethany would have such explicit evidence at her fingertips?

RACHEL

Well, you for one. You knew.

ZELDA

I knew?

RACHEL

She's one of your former students after all. Isn't she?

ZELDA

Bethany worked in my lab, fifteen years ago. *As an undergrad.*

RACHEL

Still, she was a reader for the conference. Clearly, you've been in touch. It's only natural to assume she's been keeping you abreast of her research, isn't it?

Beat.

ZELDA

Yes, and Bethany's work concerns the childbearing practices of monkeys. Not the evolutionary necessity of human menstruation. I had no idea she'd completed a phylogenic analysis of the menses of primates. Why would she? It's completely tangential to her research. She said she did it because she was curious.

RACHEL

And see—that right there. That seems suspicious to me.

ZELDA

Why would I deliberately create a competition between you and Bethany?

RACHEL

Between your biological daughter and your adopted one? I don't know. Nature versus nurture?

ZELDA

What kind of person do you think I am?

RACHEL

I have no fucking idea what kind of a person you are. You gave me away when I was six days old.

Silence.

ZELDA
hurt

I hadn't seen Bethany in fifteen years. I had no idea what specific experiments her current research entailed. But I was thrilled to find out she held a missing link. The experiment comparing the menstrual output of one species of primate to another. The experiment you thought had never been done.

RACHEL

You were *thrilled?*

ZELDA

Yes. For you. As a scientist. Thrilled that you would finally have the truth. The fact that Bethany's research found little connection between the sexual proclivity of a species and the heaviness of its menstrual flow, as you hypothesized—well, that is disappointing. But it's information you should be glad to have. If you are at all serious about this theory of yours. About evolutionary biology. About science in general. About yourself, for God's sake. If you're interested in pursuing this for any other reason than to get back at me.

Beat.

RACHEL
amazed

Is that what you think I'm doing?

ZELDA

Why did you go into this discipline?

RACHEL

I was *interested* in it.

ZELDA

See, that right there, I find suspicious. You were interested in pursuing a career in my *exact* field?

RACHEL
I didn't know it was your field. I didn't know who the hell you were.

ZELDA
So what was so "interesting" to you about evolutionary biology?

Rachel stares at Zelda.

RACHEL
When normal people want to make sense of their idiosyncratic physiology, they just look at their mother or father. But my mother and father were complete genetic strangers. So I had to study the human fucking race.

Beat.

ZELDA
That makes sense. That's just what I would have done.

RACHEL
I didn't find out who you were until I called the adoption agency two weeks ago. I thought it was a joke. I thought someone was playing a trick on me.

ZELDA
Well, I didn't know about Bethany. That's the God's honest truth.

Silence. A momentary détente.

RACHEL
I never expected it to come from a woman.

ZELDA
What?

RACHEL

The criticism. The most… injurious criticism. I expected it to come from a man. But not a woman. I thought we were all on the same team.

ZELDA

Yes, well, that was naïve of you.

RACHEL

Bethany basically accused me of misogyny. She said my hypothesis suggests a woman's sexual promiscuity is measurable by her volume of menstrual output.

ZELDA

I did try to warn you that that was one possible *mis*-interpretation of your hypothesis.

RACHEL

But you knew, *you knew*, that wasn't my intention. And yet, you said nothing.

ZELDA

What could I have said?

RACHEL

Something. Anything. You said I was brilliant. You said you *believed* in me.

ZELDA

Rachel, I introduced you. I gave you my blessing.

RACHEL

Sure, and then as soon as they started to attack me, you disappeared. I looked around the room for you. When I was up there, under siege, I tried to find you. Anything from you. A gesture. A smile. Even eye contact —

ZELDA

Really? If I had winked at you in that moment, all your problems would have evaporated?

RACHEL
desperately

Where did you go?

Beat.

ZELDA

I wasn't feeling well. I went to the bathroom.

RACHEL

You went to the bathroom. While I was up there, being broiled alive.

ZELDA

I thought you were a grown-up. I didn't realize you needed me to hold your hand.

RACHEL

Was it an emergency?

ZELDA

I beg your pardon?

RACHEL

Did you really, *really* have to go?

ZELDA

That isn't your business.

Beat.

RACHEL

When, exactly, did you go to the bathroom?

ZELDA

I'm not having this conversation.

RACHEL
Did you stay until the end of my presentation?

ZELDA
Of course.

RACHEL
So it was around the time they started to ask questions.

Zelda stares at Rachel.

RACHEL
I'm just wondering if you stayed in the room long enough to realize I was going down.

ZELDA
The only person who believes you "went down" at the conference is you! Everyone else witnessed the courageous, invigorating presentation of an exciting young talent, who *lost it* at the first whisper of criticism.

A beat.

Rachel stands, slowly.

ZELDA
Rachel, for goodness sake, sit down.

RACHEL
Go to hell.

Beat. Zelda sighs.

ZELDA
What will you do now?

Rachel doesn't answer.

ZELDA

Will you continue to refine your hypothesis or shift your concentration to something else?

Rachel stops.

RACHEL

I want to shift my concentration to bringing Bethany Gilette to her fucking knees. I've been playing the questions over and over again in my mind... and here's the thing, nobody offered up a counter-hypothesis. They poked holes in my theory, but nobody had another explanation for why women menstruate. Which means I'm still probably right. I just need to prove Bethany and her butt-licking monkeys wrong. I'm not worried. She's probably falsifying the fuck out of that data.

Beat.

ZELDA

It might be better if you didn't think of science as such a competitive sport—

RACHEL

Don't be ridiculous. Of course it is.

ZELDA

Bethany is a good scientist. You might not agree with all of her findings, but you can't just erase them. You have to be willing to hear criticism.

RACHEL

I can hear criticism.

ZELDA

Good, because there's something I need to tell you. Will you sit?

Rachel remains standing.

ZELDA

Fine. When I was in Vienna, I had the opportunity to visit the Institute of Biological Sciences where I spoke with their chief scientist who is an ex-lover of mine. I told her about your hypothesis. She—

RACHEL

She?

ZELDA

Yes. She found it fascinating, but entirely misguided. According to Marie, menstruation is not as calorically expensive as *not* menstruating. As maintaining a uterine lining at conception-ready conditions *all the time*. With all the hormones, proteins, fats, sugars required to sustain a fetus— do you know how much oxygen that endometrium requires?

RACHEL

A lot.

ZELDA

A tremendous amount. So couldn't it be more cost effective to *shed* the layer each month? Grow another one the next month. Try again?

Zelda waits for Rachel to respond. Nothing.

ZELDA

You asked why we bleed. Why our bodies don't just use water. You think it's because blood carries immune cells. But according to Marie, there's another explanation. Tiny spiral arteries weave together around the uterus each month to provide the placenta with blood if a pregnancy were to occur. When the endometrium dies and flushes out of the body, it takes the tips of these arteries with it.

RACHEL

So the blood is just waste.

ZELDA

Basically, yes.

RACHEL

That makes sense.

ZELDA

Well, there's your counter-hypothesis.

RACHEL

How old is Marie?

ZELDA

What does that have to —

RACHEL

She's your age, isn't she?

ZELDA

Yes.

RACHEL

From the generation of martyrs.

ZELDA

The generation of what?

RACHEL

"According to Marie," we women bleed each month so that, when the time comes, our fetuses can drink our blood. How noble of us. How selfless. So much better than an anti-pathogen theory, with its erotic overtones and carnal implications. Of course, everyone would much prefer a theory in which women bleed to sustain their babies rather than to protect themselves from penises. Even if it's wrong.

You fucking feminists. You're so hypocritical. You go on and on about female empowerment and all you did for us, but the truth is, you're ten times harder on us than anybody else.

Beat. Zelda will not rise to take the bait.

ZELDA

Women keep having sex well into menopause. How then do they continue to protect themselves from sperm? If menstruation is a woman's natural defense against the toxicity of sperm, why should this system shut down so many years before a woman stops having sex?

Rachel sighs.

RACHEL
tired

It shouldn't.

ZELDA

Precisely. But that doesn't mean your theory is wrong. It's just not complete.

RACHEL

The reason we don't continue to menstruate after menopause is because we are not biologically intended to live past menopause. My theory isn't wrong. Yours is.

Beat.

ZELDA

You mean it's inconvenient.

RACHEL

I mean the Grandmother Hypothesis is wrong. Don't take it personally.

ZELDA

Rachel. You don't need to destroy me to make room for yourself.

RACHEL

Destroy you? Why would I want to destroy you? You are nothing to me. You're just somebody who came before me and got it wrong.

Silence. Zelda stares at Rachel. She makes a decision to let go.

ZELDA

Maybe you're right. Maybe the Grandmother Hypothesis needs revision.

RACHEL

What?

ZELDA

Theories are mortal. Just like the people who create them. I've been waiting a long time for someone to come along and kill mine off. What a relief. You're finally here.

Beat. Rachel frowns.

RACHEL

What are you doing?

ZELDA

What do you mean?

RACHEL

Is this some sort of reverse psychology?

ZELDA

No.

RACHEL

Are you trying to get me to renounce my theory?

ZELDA

Why would you do that? You haven't even published.

Beat.

RACHEL

You're frightened of me.

ZELDA

Come again?

RACHEL

Of course you are. How did I miss that?

Zelda laughs.

ZELDA

You can't be serious.

RACHEL

That's why you got me the spot in the conference. You knew my theory wasn't ready. You knew that would happen. And you threw me up there anyway. You *wanted* it to happen. Because I scare the shit out of you.

ZELDA

Please. That's enough.

RACHEL

You stayed in that room just long enough to see me crack. And then you left because you didn't want to prolong your association with failure. I guess I really should have anticipated that. This is sort of your forte, isn't it? Abandoning your mistakes?

Zelda slaps Rachel across the face. Rachel backs away, stunned.

RACHEL

There is something wrong with you. I don't know what it is, but there is something *unnatural* about you.

Silence.

ZELDA

Forgive me.

RACHEL

How? You're not *sorry*.

Rachel turns again, to the door.

ZELDA

Don't get on the roads now. It's too late. They'll be dark and
covered with ice.

RACHEL

I'm taking the train.

ZELDA
confused

What about Dean's car?

RACHEL

He drove it home already.

ZELDA

He left you here alone? That wasn't very nice.

RACHEL

That is an amazing sentiment, coming from you.

ZELDA

Why don't you stay with me tonight? You can drive back in
the morning when it's light.

RACHEL

I'm taking the train.

> Beat.

ZELDA

That's right. You said that.

Well.

Please tell Dean I'm sorry I didn't have the chance to meet
him. Next trip, perhaps.

> Beat. Rachel doesn't respond. But she doesn't leave
> either. Instead, she turns back to the room.

RACHEL

We broke up.

ZELDA

What?

RACHEL

Dean and I broke up.

ZELDA

When?

RACHEL

After NOORB. Or maybe it was during. I don't know. He left
a note.

ZELDA

He left a *note?* What did it say?

RACHEL

He said he could tell he was no longer a priority for me.

ZELDA

Oh, Rachel. You must be angry.

RACHEL

At whom?

ZELDA

At Dean!

RACHEL

Not really. I'm angry at myself. And a little bit at you. I'm
angry at myself for *listening* to you. I should have just let him
share that stupid presentation.

Beat.

ZELDA

Who wrote the abstract?

RACHEL

That doesn't matter.

ZELDA
That's the only thing that matters.

RACHEL
No, the only thing that matters — the only thing that has ever mattered — *is Dean.*

Rachel comes back into the room.

RACHEL
In the dream I was at a rally. Like some sort of communist rally, but it was all women. We were wearing red arm bands. They hoisted a red flag. And out of nowhere, a man dressed in black appeared. He raised a gun and he shot the flag. It made a black hole in the red fabric. And as the flag fluttered, slowly, the whole thing turned black. I woke up, spooked. I woke Dean up. I told him about it. And he said, *he said,* it's a dream about sex.

ZELDA
Rachel, I could have told you that was a dream about sex.

RACHEL
But you didn't. He did. And without him, I wouldn't have thought twice about that dream. We stayed up all night together. We teased out all the possibilities and in the morning we had come up with the theory. Together. But because I listened to you and your bullshit, I wouldn't even let him share the stage —

ZELDA
Who wrote the abstract?

RACHEL
It doesn't matter!

ZELDA
Who wrote the abstract?

RACHEL

You're not *listening* to me.

ZELDA

I'm sorry things didn't work out between you and Dean. But that is just further evidence of his tremendous immaturity. He doesn't have the ability, the decency, to be happy for you and your achievements—

RACHEL

What did I achieve? I was publicly humiliated and I lost the only person who ever believed in me.

ZELDA

You believe in you.

RACHEL

What?

ZELDA

What Dean thinks doesn't matter. What I think doesn't matter. The only opinion that needs to matter to you is yours.

Silence.

RACHEL

Have you ever loved *anyone*?

Beat.

ZELDA

Yes.

RACHEL

I mean, really loved them. Enough to give up everything for them?

ZELDA

No. Because that sort of love does not exist. It is a fantasy that cowardly young women tell themselves to avoid the reality that they voluntarily fucked up their lives.

RACHEL

That isn't true.

ZELDA

If your love affair with Dean was so extraordinary, how come it fell apart so easily? Have you asked yourself that?

RACHEL

Because love is fucking magic. And like magic, you have to believe in it. You make an agreement—both of you—it's unspoken, but it's there—to put the other person first. In every decision you make. Because you know, somewhere in the deepest part of your soul, that is what will make your life worth living!

Zelda looks at her, calmly.

ZELDA

You want to know what love is? It's stress. It's just stress. Certain species with a vigorous stress response axis, whose adrenal glands release a high amount of cortisol, those are the species that fall in love often. Such as prairie voles. Sex is an act of aggression. It triggers a stress response, which makes the woman being penetrated attach to the man on top of her. Basically, love is the Stockholm syndrome, gussied up. It may sound laughable, but it's biological. I don't like it, but I respect it. I have succumbed to it in the past, but I refuse to let something so *ordinary* define me. I am smarter than a prairie vole. I have a *mind*. And I intend to use it. I thought, perhaps, you intended to use yours as well. I see now that I was wrong. Go back to Dean. Grovel. Give him a blowjob. I'm sure you'll be fine.

Beat. Rachel stares at her mother. A realization.

RACHEL

You must be so lonely. You've spent your whole life alone, with your face in a microscope.

Zelda sighs.

ZELDA

You could look at it that way. I think it's the most thrilling possible way to spend one's time. The chance that in every minute of every day you might stumble across even the smallest secret of the universe. And for a moment, this new truth will be known only to you. We are explorers, you and I. The luckiest of men.

Silence. Neither knows what to say. They are oceans apart. Rachel smiles.

ZELDA

What's so funny?

RACHEL

Charles doesn't teach the Grandmother Hypothesis.

ZELDA
confused

Who's Charles?

RACHEL

My advisor at NYU.

ZELDA

Oh. Ah, okay.

RACHEL

Charles says you couldn't find mitochondria with the Hubble telescope.

Beat.

ZELDA

Nobody could find mitochondria with a telescope.

RACHEL

It's a joke.

ZELDA

It isn't a very good one.

RACHEL

Charles says you belong to a group of women scientists who, in the eighties, thought with their vaginas.

ZELDA

My God.

RACHEL

Charles says you used some scientific voodoo to conjure a primitive matriarch from beneath the earth and give her back her powers. But she's been dead since mankind realized that sperm is the catalyst of creation. Everyone but you can clearly see she is nothing more than a rotting corpse with a crown on her head.

Silence.

ZELDA

Well. That is depressing.

RACHEL

Do you know Charles?

ZELDA

Only by reputation.

RACHEL

He did his post-doc work at Columbia.

ZELDA

Did he.

RACHEL

He had Henry Mortimer as an advisor too.

ZELDA

Henry's a very famous scientist. He advised a lot of people.

RACHEL

So you never overlapped?

ZELDA

With Charles? I don't know. What years was he there?

Beat.

RACHEL

Who's my father?

No response.

RACHEL

Is it Charles?

ZELDA

Charlie Byrne. God, no.

RACHEL

Who is it then?

ZELDA

Rachel, use your head.

RACHEL

My head says it's Charles.

ZELDA

Well, use somebody else's head then.

Beat.

RACHEL
I think you were running away from someone at Columbia.

Beat.

Henry?

Zelda just looks at her.

Henry Mortimer?

Zelda nods.

Oh my God. Henry Mortimer is my fucking father??

Zelda looks around the bar, embarrassed.

ZELDA
whispering
Keep your voice down.

RACHEL
Why didn't you just say Einstein?

ZELDA
Is it really that big a deal?

RACHEL
Are you kidding me? The Father of Hormone Replacement Therapy?

ZELDA
You do realize that all of his clinical studies were underwritten by the pharmaceutical companies, right?

RACHEL
So?

ZELDA
So, perhaps a more measured response to his historical significance—

RACHEL

The Eternal Female sold over a million copies. When has that *ever* happened to an evolutionary biologist?

ZELDA

By saying menopause was entirely avoidable!

Rachel just looks at Zelda, blankly.

ZELDA

Oh for God's sake, Rachel, he's been debunked.

RACHEL

I cannot believe Henry Mortimer is my father.

ZELDA

Doesn't it bother you that the very existence of HRT implies that a woman's body doesn't know what it's doing? That it needs to be supplemented with hormones it has naturally elected to stop producing? Just look at the word he chose to *name* it. Therapy. As if menopause was some sort of disease. It's all *marketing*. Our bodies are not sick. Estrogen is not a drug. Given in excess, it's been proven toxic.

RACHEL

So what?

ZELDA

Doesn't it bother you?

RACHEL

Not really. Does it bother you?

ZELDA

Yes, it does.

RACHEL

Maybe because his hypothesis ultimately proved more popular than yours—

ZELDA

No, you little ingrate, because I have cancer!

Silence.

RACHEL

You have what?

ZELDA

That's why I went in the bathroom during your Q & A. And that's why I was in Vienna. To receive an experimental treatment.

RACHEL

You said you went to Vienna with some dude named Michael.

ZELDA

I did. He's my oncologist.

RACHEL

You said he was your boyfriend.

ZELDA

I lied. I do that sometimes.

Beat.

RACHEL

You have cancer.

ZELDA

Yes.

RACHEL

What kind?

ZELDA

Breast.

RACHEL

What phase?

ZELDA

Three.

RACHEL

Has it spread to the lymph nodes?

ZELDA

Yes. Some.

RACHEL

That's bad.

ZELDA

I know. There's a new clinical trial happening in Vienna. It hasn't been approved by the FDA… So…

RACHEL

Is it working?

ZELDA

I don't know yet.

Beat.

ZELDA

I didn't mean to abandon you. It's just… the chemo makes me… I needed to use the bathroom.

RACHEL

I don't know what to say. I'm sorry.

Beat. Zelda doesn't believe her.

ZELDA

Thank you.

Silence.

RACHEL

Did you take estrogen?

                    ZELDA

Yes.

                    RACHEL

When?

                    ZELDA

After you were born.

                    RACHEL

But you were so young.

    Beat.

                    ZELDA

I had a hysterectomy.

                    RACHEL

Why?

                    ZELDA

There were... complications with my placenta during my
delivery. I couldn't stop bleeding. They had to remove my
uterus.

                    RACHEL

During your delivery with me.

                    ZELDA

Yes.

                    RACHEL

That's why you never had any other children.

                    ZELDA

Yes.

                    RACHEL

And now you have cancer.

    *Beat. Rachel suddenly drops her forehead to the table
    with a bang.*

ZELDA
alarmed

It isn't your fault.

> *Rachel sits up, but something's wrong. She's breathing heavily.*

ZELDA

Are you okay?

> *Rachel shakes her head.*

ZELDA

What's the matter?

RACHEL

I can't breathe.

ZELDA

Why not?

> *Rachel starts to hyperventilate.*

RACHEL

I can't breathe.

ZELDA

Rachel. Rachel! Look at me. You're fine.

RACHEL
hoarsely

My throat's closing up.

ZELDA

Then breathe through your nose.

RACHEL
hoarsely

Can you call an ambulance?

No.

RACHEL
hoarsely
I can't breathe.

ZELDA
If you can speak, you can breathe.

RACHEL
gasping
It might take them a while to get here!

Zelda stands, gets behind Rachel and rubs her back.

ZELDA
Just concentrate on breathing. In through your nose. Out through your mouth. Ready? In... two... three. Out... two... three. In through your nose, out through your mouth. In... two... three. Out... two... three...

Rachel breathes as Zelda keeps chanting instructions. She slowly starts to calm down. Finally, she stops hyperventilating.

ZELDA
Better?

Rachel nods.

RACHEL
That breathing thing works.

ZELDA
Lamaze.

RACHEL
What?

ZELDA

Never mind. That looked exhausting. Let's get you something to eat. Can you order anything here?

Zelda signals the bartender offstage.

ZELDA

Food, please. And some water.

Turning back to Rachel.

ZELDA

Oh no, you're crying again.

RACHEL

I miss Dean.

Rachel puts her head back on the table.

ZELDA

I know. I know. It gets easier.

RACHEL

You don't know that. You've never been in love.

ZELDA

I've heard it does. From trustworthy people.

Zelda again reaches out a hand to touch Rachel's head, and again, she pulls it away.

ZELDA

Has this happened before?

RACHEL
into the table

Yes.

ZELDA

You get panic attacks?

RACHEL

Sometimes.

ZELDA

What does it feel like?

RACHEL

One moment I'm fine and the next, this thing starts
happening to me and I can't make it stop.

ZELDA

I can tell you how.

Rachel looks up.

ZELDA

Next time this starts to happen, I want you to try something.
Instead of thinking about how to make it stop, say to
yourself, "This is coming out of me. There's something in
this situation that is upsetting me and this is my body's way
of letting me know that I'm scared."

Rachel stares at Zelda.

RACHEL

That is absolutely not going to work.

ZELDA

Try it.

RACHEL

I feel like I'm *choking to death.*

ZELDA

Just try it. "It's not happening to me, it's coming out of me."

RACHEL

Yeah, yeah. I got it.

ZELDA

It's a way to take back psychological control.

I used to get them too.

RACHEL

I really don't think we're having the same experience.

Zelda looks at Rachel, sadly.

ZELDA

What happened to make this generation so afraid?

RACHEL

Oh, I don't know, our parents?

Beat. Zelda looks up at the bar.

ZELDA
re: the popcorn

Ah. Splendid.

*Zelda gets up and returns with two big bowls of popcorn.
She sets one down in front of Rachel and one in front of
herself.*

The women eat popcorn in silence.

RACHEL

So, you and Henry Mortimer. How did that happen?

ZELDA

Have you ever slept with one of your professors?

RACHEL

No!

ZELDA

Really? And why not?

RACHEL

That's against the rules.

ZELDA

When I was young there were no rules.

I think we created those rules.

RACHEL

How long did it last?

ZELDA

On-and-off again for most of my graduate and post-doc work.

RACHEL

Then what happened?

ZELDA

Nothing. We drifted apart.

RACHEL

Why did you leave Columbia?

ZELDA

I got a grant.

Beat. Another penny drops.

RACHEL

I happened.

ZELDA

That wasn't it.

RACHEL

Of course. It's so obvious. You got pregnant. He was probably married. So you had to disappear.

Beat.

surprised

That's your theory?

RACHEL

Am I right?

ZELDA

He *was* married.

RACHEL

I knew it. Did he ask you to have an abortion?

ZELDA

No.

RACHEL

Did he kick you out of the program?

ZELDA

No.

RACHEL

Well, what did he do when you told him?

ZELDA

I never told him.

    Beat.

RACHEL
surprised

You never told him?

ZELDA

No. I got a grant to study the Hadza. So I left.

RACHEL

What do you mean? You just took off?

                    ZELDA
Pretty much.

                    RACHEL
Did you leave him a note?

                    ZELDA
I sent him a postcard. From Dar es Salaam.

                    RACHEL
What did it say?

                    ZELDA
"Safe upon the solid rock the ugly houses stand:
Come and see my shining palace built upon the sand!"

        Beat.

                    RACHEL
Edna?

        Zelda nods.

                    RACHEL
Seriously?

                    ZELDA
I like her!

I didn't know what to write.

I was young.

                    RACHEL
Did your oncologist really give you that plaque? The one in
your office?

                    ZELDA
No.

                    RACHEL
So who's M?

Mortimer.

Henry.

Zelda nods.

Jesus. It sounds like he was crazy about you.

Beat.

Suddenly, Zelda can't sit down anymore. She gets up and begins to move around. Rachel watches her. Fascinated.

Did you live with them?

Who?

The Hadza.

Oh. For a bit.

While you were *pregnant*?

confused

Yes.

Weren't you scared?

Of what?

RACHEL

That something would go wrong and you'd be stuck there —

ZELDA

No. I figured my body knew how to make a baby.

RACHEL

I would have been terrified.

ZELDA

They were actually very kind to me. Shared their water, their honey, their monkey meat.

RACHEL

You ate monkey meat?

ZELDA

Occasionally.

RACHEL

During my gestation?

ZELDA

Only during your first trimester.

RACHEL

Their genetic code is only a few chromosomes off of ours! No wonder I'm such a disaster.

ZELDA

You're not a disaster.

RACHEL

Yes, I am.

ZELDA

I don't think so.

RACHEL

You're not allowed to think so. You're my mother.

Beat. Zelda is touched.

ZELDA

Even if I weren't. Even if I were just another scientist who attended the NOORB conference, I would think you were a strong young mind with a bright future ahead of you.

RACHEL

That's because you went to the bathroom. Every other scientist at that conference thinks I'm an embarrassment. I can't go back to my lab —

ZELDA
alarmed

Why not?

RACHEL

I can't face it. Dean will be there. My career is ruined.

ZELDA

Your career is not ruined.

RACHEL

I suppose I could teach —

ZELDA
confused

Teach?

RACHEL

At a high school level —

ZELDA

Rachel —

RACHEL

Or maybe I should go back to school for something else. Medicine maybe. I could be a doctor. I already know most of the science —

ZELDA

RACHEL! You are going back to the lab.

RACHEL

No, I can't.

ZELDA

Are you crazy?

RACHEL

Everybody is going to laugh at me.

ZELDA

So what if they laugh at you?

RACHEL

It's a horrible feeling.

ZELDA

Of course it is. And you have those horrible feelings — you experience that failure — that sense of the embarrassment — of loss — so that when you come back again, swinging hard, and you do finally knock some of the pins down — or maybe even, one day, all of the pins — you will know it was no accident. That you knew what you were doing and you did it well. Rachel, your youth… your horrible, burdensome, terrifying youth will not last forever. I promise you. It will be over the moment you've finally started to enjoy it. And after that, everything goes. Your eggs first. Your body next. Your mind, *even your mind*, will one day leave you. We end our lives like hollow shells along the beach, rattling around as the water wears us white, indistinguishable from our neighbors. *That* is what you have to look forward too.

You want to beat them? The ones who've laughed at you? I'll tell you how. It's very simple, really. Just survive. Go back to your laboratory. Put your face back to the microscope, keep your eyes open, and stay there. I promise you, if you do that — you will win your war.

RACHEL

It sounds like a long fight.

ZELDA

It is.

RACHEL

What about the times that I can't be in the lab? Because they've locked it? Because it's, say, Christmas? I've always spent the holidays with Dean's family. What am I supposed to do now?

Pause.

Zelda takes a deep breath. This isn't easy for her to ask.

ZELDA
quietly

Come with me.

RACHEL
surprised

You?

ZELDA

I go up to this little inn in New Hampshire. It usually snows too hard to do much of anything, but I can show you how to tap a maple tree.

RACHEL

You're kidding.

ZELDA

You should come.

RACHEL

To spend Christmas with you. Just the two of us.

ZELDA

It will be fun.

Beat. Rachel stares at Zelda.

I'll think about it.

ZELDA

excited

In the town, there are the most charming little antique stores.
I've always wanted to spend an afternoon looking through
them. I don't know why I haven't. Antiquing just seemed
like something people do together. Maybe we could find you
an old Singer sewing machine table. Have you ever seen one
of those? I had one as a girl. It was the perfect size for a
child's desk.

Rachel is getting increasingly uncomfortable.

RACHEL

Yeah, maybe.

ZELDA

We don't have to. Not everyone likes antiques.

RACHEL

No, if I come, we should go.

ZELDA

"If you come."

RACHEL

I was just thinking... it wouldn't be so hard to get a key to
the lab over Christmas.

I bet they'd leave the power on if I ask them to. I know that's
probably not considered good for my psyche or whatever,
but it's just... I mean, if your friend Marie is right, and the
anti-pathogen theory of menstruation is wrong, well then, I
don't really have time to take a holiday. I've got to get back
to the lab and figure something else out.

ZELDA

You have plenty of time.

RACHEL

Not really. You had the Grandmother Hypothesis by the time you were my age, didn't you? Isn't that why you gave me up?

ZELDA

What?

RACHEL

You went into the bush. You saw how those primitive women passed their kids around, to their mothers, their sisters, it takes a village, blah, blah, blah. You had a breakthrough. And you knew it was good. Good enough to carry you home. Good enough to get you tenure. But you also knew that it would be hard to take seriously a single woman who walked out of the bush with a radical hypothesis and a fatherless child. And since you never really wanted the baby to begin with —

ZELDA

Stop it.

RACHEL

What's wrong?

ZELDA

You don't have the slightest idea what you're talking about.

RACHEL

angry

Maybe not. But spare me your *Little House on the Prairie* fantasies. Antiquing? You gave up *your baby*. I just want to work through Christmas.

Beat.

ZELDA

Then I'll come to you. I have an old friend with an apartment in the city. She's on sabbatical; I'm sure I could stay there.

RACHEL

Why?

ZELDA

Why not? I'll make us a goose.

We're family, Rachel.

Rachel has something she needs to say. She takes a deep breath.

RACHEL

You made a choice, Zelda. I understand why you did it, but you can't take it back. You are the woman who gave birth to me. You are not my mother. I don't have to hold your hand while you die.

Silence.

RACHEL

I'm sorry.

ZELDA

Don't be. You're protecting yourself. Don't ever apologize for that.

Silence. Neither woman knows what to say.

RACHEL

Do you have anyone?

ZELDA

What do you mean?

RACHEL

Who can... be with you?

ZELDA

Oh. Of course. I have friends.

RACHEL

What about your mother?

ZELDA

She's dead.

RACHEL

When did she die?

ZELDA

When I was your age.

Beat.

RACHEL

How did she die?

Beat.

ZELDA

Breast cancer.

RACHEL

Shit.

ZELDA

There's a test you can take. It's called the BRCA 1. To find out just how high the genetic risk is.

RACHEL

What am I supposed to do with that information? Get a prophylactic mastectomy?

ZELDA

I would take the test, if I were you.

Silence.

RACHEL

What about Henry?

Zelda frowns.

ZELDA

I don't think there was any breast cancer in his family.

RACHEL

No, I mean, what about Henry — for you.

Beat.

ZELDA

For me?

RACHEL

Does he know you're... that you have...?

ZELDA

I haven't spoken to Henry since...

I hear about him from time to time, of course. Mostly from my graduate students who have moved on to post-docs in his lab.

He sounds happy.

Silence.

There's something still bothering Rachel.

RACHEL

Here's what I can't figure out. In science, every phenomenon is explainable from two perspectives. The how and the why. I understand how I happened. I still don't understand why.

Beat. Zelda doesn't respond.

RACHEL

Why didn't you just have an abortion?

ZELDA

I didn't want to.

RACHEL

Are you religious?

ZELDA

No, I'm Darwinian.

Silence.

RACHEL

Did you get pregnant on purpose?

ZELDA

That's quite an accusation.

RACHEL

Not if you loved him. Really loved him. And you wanted to have a child with him. Because that's what women do. We fall in love with men and we think "Wouldn't it be nice to have his babies?"

Silence.

RACHEL

It makes sense. Maybe you thought that was the only way to get Henry to leave his wife but he wouldn't. So you fled. All the way to Africa. Just to have some space to think.

Beat. Zelda is deeply disappointed in Rachel.

ZELDA

You're being horrible, Rachel.

RACHEL

Why? What's so horrible about it? Why can't you just admit it, Zelda? *You fell in love.* For one moment in your life, you wanted something beyond your illustrious career.

That's why I was born.

Beat.

Am I right?

Zelda clears her throat.

ZELDA

You're a good scientist, sweetheart. You're completely insane, but you're fearless, so you'll go far.

RACHEL
annoyed

Am I right?

ZELDA

Henry had already left his wife for me. We were living together when I went to Tanzania.

Beat.

RACHEL

Then I don't understand.

ZELDA

I had an idea, Rachel. A hypothesis that argues women are more evolutionarily important than men. And I had a boyfriend. Twenty years my senior. My professor. A man I revered. *And yes, loved.* Whose entire career had been built on the opposite assumption.

I could publish my hypothesis. Or I could bury it. And go on with him. Probably grow old with him.

I chose to publish it.

RACHEL

Why?

ZELDA

ferocious

How could I not?

RACHEL

I would never have had the guts to do the same thing.

ZELDA

What the hell are you talking about? You just did.

Beat.

RACHEL

Fuck.

Silence. And from the silence, comes the question of the play.

RACHEL

Was it worth it?

Zelda thinks.

ZELDA

Some days, yes. Some days, no.

Silence.

RACHEL

Why didn't you keep me?

Beat.

ZELDA

I wish I had.

Silence.

Want to hear something funny?

Okay.

They told me I was adopted when I was around five, and for years after that, every time my mother tried to get me to do something I didn't want to do, I would say to her, you're not my real mother. My real mother is a queen and I am a princess.

Beat.

That is funny.

Rachel stares at Zelda. Then she puts her head down on the table. She's suddenly so tired.

Is my whole life going to be this hard?

It depends what you do with it. It will either be hard or boring. You get to pick.

What do I do now?

Get back to your lab.

And work on what?

Your hypothesis.

                    RACHEL

It's broken.

                    ZELDA

No, Rachel. It isn't complete.

                    RACHEL

I don't know how to fix it.

        Beat.

                    ZELDA

You'll figure it out.

        Silence. Rachel sighs.

                    RACHEL

I should really be going. I wanted to catch the last train back
to Penn Station.

        Zelda nods.

                    ZELDA

I'll get the check.

                    RACHEL

I already paid for the drinks.

                    ZELDA

What about the popcorn?

                    RACHEL

It's free.

                    ZELDA

Free?

        Zelda looks around.

                    ZELDA

I'll have to remember this place.

They both stand. They don't know what to do. Zelda puts out her hand to shake.

Rachel steps forward and gives her mother a tentative hug.

They separate. Rachel heads towards the door.

Zelda sits down again, slowly.

Rachel turns back.

> **RACHEL**
> *alarmed*

Are you okay?

> **ZELDA**

Fine.

> **RACHEL**

Are you coming?

Zelda shakes her head.

> **ZELDA**

I'm going to stay here a bit.

A moment.

> **RACHEL**

That's a hell of a theory, Zelda. The Grandmother Hypothesis.

> **ZELDA**

I know.

> **RACHEL**

What was it like? To dream it up at 28?

> **ZELDA**

I don't remember. All I really remember from that point in my life — is chaos.

Beat.

RACHEL

Some days I'm so sad, I wish I were dead.

ZELDA

I have those days.

RACHEL

I don't know what to do about them.

ZELDA

Ride them through.

Freeze on the tableau.

End of Play